# POCKET PRAYERS
## *for* WOMEN

# Finding
# *Angels*
## *When You Need Them*

**pil** Publications International, Ltd.

**Marie D. Jones** is the author of several best-selling nonfiction books and a contributing writer on numerous inspirational works, including *Echoes of Love: Sisters, Mother, Grandmother, Friends, Graduation,* and *Wedding; A Mother's Daily Prayer Book;* and *When You Lose Someone You Love: A Year of Comfort.* She can be reached at www.mariedjones.com.

**Additional contributors:** Anne Broyles, Christine A. Dallman, June Eaton, Lain Chroust Ehmann, Jennifer Huston, Randy Petersen, Ellen F. Pill, Carol McAdoo Rehme, Carol Smith, Carol Stigger, Anna Trimiew, Natalie Walker Whitlock, Kelly Womer

Louis Weber, CEO
Publications International, Ltd.
7373 North Cicero Avenue
Lincolnwood, Illinois 60712

ISBN-13: 978-1-4508-6137-3
ISBN-10: 1-4508-6137-7

Manufactured in China.

8 7 6 5 4 3 2 1

# Angels Are Everywhere

Humans like to feel that they are in control of their lives. But it's comforting to know that God sends his angels to guide and protect us.

*Pocket Prayers for Women: Finding Angels When You Need Them* is a devotional of prayers asking God to send his angels when we most need love and support. The Bible passages and inspirational quotes included help us express our love for the Lord and his heavenly hosts.

Best of all, *Pocket Prayers for Women: Finding Angels When You Need Them* is small enough to fit inside a purse or briefcase, making it easy to take advantage of the privilege of talking with God and your guardian angels every day.

# An Abundance of Angels

*Bless the Lord, O you his angels,*
*you mighty ones who do his bidding,*
*obedient to his spoken word.*

Psalm 103:20

*L*ord, I know that you simply cannot be everywhere at once, so you made angels to help you spread your loving grace upon the earth. Thank you for blessing my life with an abundance of angels in the form of friends and family members who love and care for me. They fill my life with joy and give me wings to follow my dreams.

# Take My Hand

*Behold, I send an Angel before thee, to keep thee in the way, and to bring thee into the place which I have prepared.*

Exodus 23:20 KJV

Father God, teach me to trust your protection. It's so hard sometimes to find my way home. The nights get dark. The clouds hide the stars. If I could learn to hold the hands of your angels, I know you would lead me all the way.

*Angels are everywhere, waiting to help us through the hardest of times. All we need to do is ask for their help and believe we will receive it.*

# Believe in Miracles

*Are not all angels ministering spirits sent
to serve those who will inherit salvation?*

Hebrews 1:14 NIV

*L*ord, in times of weakness and
doubt, help me remember that
you are always capable of miracles. Keep
me ever alert for visits from the angels
you send to protect and guide me. May I
receive them with a joyous and grateful
heart and then pass on the blessings to
others who need their comfort. Amen.

# My New Beginning

Today is my new beginning,
The past is over and done,
However I got to this point,
From here I can only move on.
Though the road ahead may be rocky,
And the future I cannot see,
I'll walk with my head held high,
With angels on each side of me.
Today is my new beginning,
And as I depart, I will pray,
That God will bless my journey,
And guide me each step of the way.

*A new beginning, like the breath of an
angel, makes the air a little sweeter and
the world seem full of hope.*

# Light and Free

*I will exult in the God of my salvation.
God, the Lord, is my strength; he makes my
feet like the feet of a deer, and makes me
tread upon the heights.*

Habakkuk 3:18–19

God, I feel so light and free today.
Everything is coming together, and
the way ahead seems so clear. I've had
so many issues lately with relationships
and family, finances and work, and for a
while I felt trapped in a fog. I love these
mornings when the sun is shining and
the birds are singing and all is well in
my world again. I thank you for all the
blessings you have given me and those
yet to come. I know life will once again

throw rocks in my path, but it's times like this when I am reminded that not only can I handle them, I can also learn from each and every rock and become a happier, stronger person as a result. Thank you, God, for being the wind beneath my wings.

*Isn't it funny how when we stop and take the time to recognize all the good in our lives, it leads to more and more good? Blessings beget more blessings, and gratitude begets more to be grateful for!*

# When I Picture an Angel

*Suddenly an angel of the Lord appeared
and a light shone…*

Acts 12:7

When I think of angels, I think of floating, celestial beings. I think of angels as beings who have only good thoughts, never bad. I see them surrounded by an eternal glow and always pleasant and completely centered. I picture them with such a sense of purpose, so connected to their reason for being that they never lose their way. I see angels as the kind of beings that I would like to be.

# Let Me Be an Angel

*For this light within you produces only*
*what is good and right and true.*

Ephesians 5:9 NLT

God in heaven, let me be an angel
to someone today. Just as you have
blessed my life with people who love
and cherish me, let me be a light of love
that shines upon someone who needs me.
I have received the gift of angels, now
allow me to give and be one in return.

*If you want to be an angel for another*
*person, you don't need wings and a*
*halo—just a loving attitude. Being aware*
*of other people's needs, fears, dreams, and*
*heartaches, you can reach out as a loving*
*presence. You don't need to solve their*
*problems—you just need to offer yourself.*

11

# Wings of Light

Wings of light surround me,
And I am enlightened.
Wings of love enfold me,
And I am comforted.
Angels guide my journey,
And I am directed.
Angels keep me safe from harm,
And I am protected.

Arms so strong lift me,
And I am emboldened.
Arms so soft hold me,
And I am at peace.
Angels grant me mercy,
And I am redeemed.
Angels walk beside me,
And I am esteemed.

Songs of joy fill me,
And I am enchanted.
Songs of love envelop me,
And I am empowered.
Angels sing above me,
And I am adored.
Angels chant in glory,
And I am restored.

# Your Suffering Servant

*O Lord my God, I cried to you for help,*
*and you have healed me.*

Psalm 30:2

Father, it's not always clear to
me why suffering comes. But I
do know that whenever I suffer, you
are close at hand. I can see you in the
kindness you deliver to me through your
angels. Some angels are strangers, some
are friends, and some are unseen, but
all remind me that you see me, that you
care for me, and that you are with me.

*Thank you, angels, for all the caring*
*things you do. Thanks for being so faithful*
*and seeing me through times of struggle*
*and despair. I feel more carefree just*
*knowing you are there.*

# A Stormy Path

When life's winds toss me upon the waves of uncertainty and doubt, when the tempest beats me upon rocks of guilt and self-pity, when my pitiful heart yearns for love I cannot find, when the darkness seems darker and the night longer, some unseen hand reaches down, and with a strength and tenderness I cannot comprehend, pulls me back into the light.

*Through strife or storm or darkest night,*
*my angel is there to show me God's light.*

# Guided and Guarded

*Blessed are those who trust in the Lord,*
*whose trust is the Lord.*

Jeremiah 17:7

Dear God, I want to thank you for my guardian angel—my rock and the column I can always lean on. I may be short on trust of the people in my world sometimes, but I know that I can count on my angel to be there with love and support. I know that through your angels, you will always protect me and guide me through each day and night so that I am never truly alone. For that I am so thankful.

# Watching from Above

Do they sit and watch us, these angels of which we are unaware? Do they lie on a cloud, heads on their hands, and peek at our world? I think I can see them sometimes if I look up and squint really hard. I think I can hear them sometimes—celestial murmurs that accompany our hardships and will one day lead us home.

*When we are feeling alone, assailed by outside forces, unsure of which way to go, it is comforting to think of angels watching over us, providing celestial support and guidance.*

# Send Me an Angel

*The Lord ... will send his angel with you*
*and make your way successful.*

Genesis 24:40

Lord, please send me an angel to
guide me and guard me, to lead
and direct me, to comfort and hold me.
Send me an angel who knows what
my heart needs most and always has
the solutions to my most challenging
problems. Send me an angel to walk
with me and hold my hand as I tread the
rocky road of life. Send me an angel soon.

*Angels help us believe in the things we*
*cannot see and understand the things we*
*can. Angels give us the faith and wisdom*
*to know that all things are possible.*

# Angels in Disguise

In this day and age, angels are more likely to appear in street clothes than in long white robes and halos. A neighbor who offers sound advice, a mentor who shows us how to live well, a friend who comforts us—all may be angels. If we are open to the possibility that God will use those around us to guide our way, then we may benefit from the direction our earthly angels give. We may not hear harps playing, but in hindsight, we may give thanks for God's angels on earth.

*Not all angels are in disguise. Look closer. You might recognize someone you know.*

# Furry Angels

*The righteous know the needs
of their animals...*

Proverbs 12:10

God, how I adore my pets, for they love me unconditionally. Like furry little angels, they love me even at my worst and are my constant and faithful companions through life's ups and downs. Every pet I've ever been blessed with has taught me so much about being in the present moment and taking life as it is and as it comes. They have been some of my greatest teachers, and I am so thankful for the creatures you have sent my way. May I learn to love as they do: without hesitation and with a wide-open heart. Amen.

*Thank you, God, for all the animals that have helped us feel closer to you and your creation. Keep them safe, these trusted innocents that calm our lives and show us love. Help them find their way home if they are lost. Help them hear the voices of those who will care for them. Protect them from every unsafe place.*

# Simple Faith

"There are no such things as angels,"
Say educated minds,
Those who have the eyes to see
But to the truth are blind.

"There are no such things as angels,"
Say the learned and the wise,
And all those who see the world
Through jaded, skeptical eyes.

"There are no such things as angels,"
The pragmatist replies
As well as the doubting masses
Who on intellect rely.

But I believe in angels
And in miracles and love,
All it takes is simple faith
And blessings from above.

# You'll See It
# When You Believe It!

*Have you believed because you have seen
me? Blessed are those who have not seen
and yet have come to believe.*

John 20:29

God, thank you for the little things
that restore my faith and make me
believe in the goodness of life again. I can
sometimes get stuck in negative thinking,
but I know I can count on my loved ones
to help dig me out of any rut, no matter
how deep and hopeless it might seem.

*The ignorant say they will believe in
angels only when they see them. The wise
understand that they will see angels only
when they believe in them.*

# A Grateful Prayer for My Support System

*Some friends play at friendship but a true friend sticks closer than one's nearest kin.*

Proverbs 18:24

Lord, you've given me a great team of helpers, and I'm exceedingly thankful. Where would I be without them? They seem to know my needs before I do, and they jump to meet them. I know you've instilled in them the gifts

24

of caring, encouragement, hospitality, and healing, and they're using those gifts as you intended—to show your love to others, including me. For that, I am thankful to you and to them.

But there's not much I can do to pay them back, Lord. They'd probably refuse a reward anyway. So I ask that you shower them with blessings, just as they have blessed me. Give them joy and peace in rich supply, and let your love continue to flow to them, through them, and within them. Amen.

> *We cannot part with our friends;*
> *we cannot let our angels go.*
> —Ralph Waldo Emerson

# The Kindness of Strangers

*Do not neglect to show hospitality to strangers, for by doing that some have entertained angels without knowing it.*

Hebrews 13:2

God, we are so often buried in our cell phones and electronic gadgets that we rarely talk to strangers anymore. How rare it is these days that we stop and say hello, offer a smile, or engage in small talk. I pray that I may never ignore the kindness of the strangers who reach out to me and that I may reach out to them as well, offering what little joy I can to help make their day a bit brighter. Lord, let me be an angel to a stranger today. Amen.

# The Gift Is in the Present

*So do not worry about tomorrow, for tomorrow will bring worries of its own. Today's trouble is enough for today.*

Matthew 6:34

God, I have always thought that my guardian angels were living things, like friends and family and my pets. But lately I've been receiving guidance everywhere I look: in a quote I see on a social-networking site or an email a friend sends with an inspiring image. Sometimes I'll open a book and turn to just the right passage that I need to read. And then I realize that angels are everywhere when I allow myself to see them. Thank you, God!

# Seeking Your Angels

*For he will command his angels*
*concerning you to guard you in all*
*your ways. On their hands they will bear*
*you up, so that you will not dash*
*your foot against a stone.*

Psalm 91:11–12

We're seldom, if ever, truly "in this alone." In the midst of trouble, we may feel dreadfully lonely, but healing rarely comes without a little or a lot of help from outside—from those people in our lives who act as our earthly guardian angels extending God's help and love.

Seeking your personal angels might literally mean going out and looking for the right person to help with your particular problem. Just as often, though, it means learning to recognize the angels who are already knocking at your door. Pain and sorrow can blind us to the compassionate friends nearby who are eager and able to help us on the road to recovery. If you're ready to seek healing, take a good look around. Your earthly angel might be standing right in front of you.

*Recognizing the presence of angels around you can feel like walking from the shadows into the warmth of sunshine. Suddenly, you feel the nourishment that comes from someone taking the time to look out for you and you alone.*

# God's Merciful Messengers

*Then Peter... said,*
*"Now I am sure that the Lord has sent*
*his angel and rescued me..."*

Acts 12:11

Heavenly Father, thank you for your holy angels, both those in heaven and those here on earth. They make life more bearable in times of trouble, and they add to our joy in good times. Keep us always in your sight, Lord. When we stumble, send your merciful messengers to pick us up. When we are lost, send them to light the way home.

*God sends his angels to hold us up so we*
*don't stumble in the darkness.*

30

# Thank You for My Angels

*D*ear God,
I am so thankful for the angels of light who guide my journey and for the angels of wisdom who whisper to me what I need to know.

I am so thankful for the angels of joy who remind me of the happiness in my life.

And I am so thankful for the guardian angel who is always with me, keeping me safe. Amen.

# What a Wonderful World!

*They shall again live beneath my shadow,*
*they shall flourish as a garden;*
*they shall blossom like a vine,*
*their fragrance shall be like*
*the wine of Lebanon.*

Hosea 14:7

*S*ometimes, I wake up in the morning, Lord, and the first I do is think about all the things on my To Do list and stress about bills and family and

work. But then I hear the gentle call of a bird or feel the breeze on my skin, and I realize I am so blessed to be alive! The world is such a magical place, filled with beauty and love. When I set my focus on the beauty and love around me, the stressful things lose their power, and I realize that life is about so much more than just plodding through each day. It's about living and loving and being in a world full of miracles. Thank you, Lord, for such a wonderful world that's teeming with angels in the form of birds and breezes and beautiful things!

*Life is what you make of it.
It can be a lovely garden or
a bed of weeds. Look for the beauty
in everything and you will find it.*

# An Angel for All Seasons

*L*oving God, help us sense your angelic messengers whenever, wherever, and however they come to us. In the darkness of winter, the brightness of spring, the abundance of summer, and the transitions of autumn, may we expect to be visited by your heavenly beings. And when these visits happen, may our eyes be open and our gratitude heartfelt.

*There is no one time or place*
*When angels can appear.*
*They come when needed,*
*Filled with grace*
*To those who God holds dear.*

# Surrounded by Angels

*Be strong and bold; have no fear or dread
of them, because it is the Lord your God
who goes with you; he will not fail you
or forsake you.*

Deuteronomy 31:6

The angels in my life are often very familiar in form. When I was sick, I thought an angel touched my forehead with a cool cloth, but it was my mother. When I was afraid, I thought an angel comforted me, but it was my brother. When I was alone, I thought an angel sat beside me, but it was my friend. Looking back, I think I was right the first time.

*The unlikeliest people harbor halos
underneath their hats.*

# Angel Friends

I believe in angels.
    They're around me every day,
I see them in a mother's touch
And in a child at play.

I see them in a neighbor's wave
And in an old friend's call,
In a martyr's heroic deed
And in a favor small.

I've heard one in a friend's "hello"
And in a newborn's cry,
In the rustle of the leaves
And in a lullaby.

They're in a loved one's legacy
And in a young child's might,
They're in the colors of the sky
And in a starry night.

I've seen one in a stranger's smile
And in a lover's glance,
In an act of selflessness
And in a second chance.

I see them in a brother's arms
And in a sister's care,
I hear them in a baby's laugh
And in a small child's prayer.

Yes, I believe in angels,
And I know that they are true,
Messengers and guardians,
Angel friends like you.

# A Compassionate Heart

*As God's chosen ones, holy and beloved,*
*clothe yourselves with compassion,*
*kindness, humility, meekness, and patience.*

Colossians 3:12

*L*ord, help me to have a more compassionate heart toward those I meet today. Whether they are positive or negative in spirit, guide me to deal with each of them as I myself would want to be treated, remembering that we are all human and are all capable of our ups and downs. Have my guardian angel remind me to react from the highest place within me, not the lowest, and to strive to be as good to them as you are to me. Thank you, God.

# Open My Eyes

God, help me recognize the angels in my life, especially those who come in the form of people I meet. Sometimes, I forget to smile at a stranger or exchange a pleasantry with a store clerk, yet they, too, could be angels. Remind me to keep my eyes and my heart open to the angels that are part of my daily life, always ready to offer a loving word or a kind gesture.

*Life is short and we have never too much time for gladdening the hearts of those who are traveling the dark journey with us. Oh be swift to love, make haste to be kind.*

—Henri Frederic Amiel

# A Prayer for the Brokenhearted

*Hope deferred makes the heart sick,*
*but a desire fulfilled is a tree of life.*

Proverbs 13:12

*L*oving God,
My heart is breaking and I don't know what to do. Please send me an angel to light my way and help me see past the dark clouds of despair to a day when the sun will shine again. Please heal my heart so that I can experience true love with the special someone you have chosen just for me. Thank you. Amen.

# Restore My Soul

*For God alone my soul waits in silence,*
*for my hope is from him. He alone is*
*my rock and my salvation, my fortress;*
*I shall not be shaken.*

Psalm 62:5–6

*G*race of my heart, I turn to you
when I am feeling lost and alone.
You restore me with strength and
hope and the courage to face a new
day. You bless me with joy and angels
who comfort me through trials and
tribulations. You direct my thoughts,
guide my actions, and temper my words.
You give me the patience and kindness
I need to be good. Grace of my heart,
I turn to you. Amen.

# This Too Shall Pass

*Rejoice in hope, be patient in suffering,*
*persevere in prayer.*

Romans 12:12

*L*ord, we both know that patience is not one of my strong suits, but I feel so tense and anxious when things don't happen right away. I pray for peace and understanding as I wait for things to change. As I deal with what lies ahead, send me an angel to watch over me and keep my head on straight and my heart in the right place. I know miracles are right around the corner. I just need a little extra loving care right now until I get there.

# Lead the Way!

Heavenly Father, I think about the moments in my life when you have changed me. I think about the words that gave me a new perspective— a new direction. I think about the angels who stepped into my life and were used by you to show me the way. I think about all these things, and I am grateful. I think about all these moments, and I am filled with confidence that you have led me on my way.

*Life is beyond our control. That is precisely why angels guard us and guide us.*

# Your Heavenly Embrace

Though I cannot see you, angel dear,
I know that you are there.
Though I cannot hear you speak,
I sense you loud and clear.
For in my heart I recognize
The pattern of your call.
And in your wings I've found
A gentle place to fall.

Should I attempt to see you, angel dear,
I know that I will fail.
Should I attempt to pin you down,
I know I won't prevail.
For in my soul I've come to know
Your presence is discerned.
And through my faith I understand
That mercy must be earned.

If ever I am lonely, angel dear,
I know you're close at hand.
If ever I am frightened,
I know that by me you will stand.
For in the quiet of the night,
I sense God's loving grace
And rest in the peaceful comfort
Of your heavenly embrace.

*Love finds us all, one way or another.*
*Love gives us reason and hope.*
*Love wraps its wings around our weakness*
*and carries us all the way home.*

45

# Thanks for Understanding

*Great is our Lord, and abundant in power;*
*his understanding is beyond measure.*

Psalm 147:5

Dear God, I'm sorry if I get frustrated or upset with my guardian angel these days. I know I must not always be the easiest person to be a guardian angel for. It's just that I'm having a hard time right now. And I sometimes forget how truly blessed I am and how good you are to me. I hope you and my guardian angel will be patient with me, and help see me through to better times. Thank you for understanding.

# Protector of All

*Cast your cares on the Lord and
he will sustain you; he will never let
the righteous be shaken.*

Psalm 55:22 NIV

*L*ord, you send your angels to us
each day when we need them
most. We thank you for the protection,
reassurance, and blessings they offer in
your name. Please continue to shower us
with these daily reminders of your great
love for us and keep us safely tucked
beneath the shadow of angel wings.

*When life seems darkest and we feel lost
and alone, that's when we are surrounded
by angels who care for us. All we need to
do is open our hearts to see them reaching
out to us with love.*

# Spanning Heaven and Earth

Halos and wings and harps and strings. Is that an angel's world? Are their streets made of gold, adorned with clockless cathedrals, surrounding a celestial park? Not for guardian angels. These are the beings spanning the beauty of heaven and the sometimes harsh reality of earth. They are the ones sweeping through town at the speed of humans, following their charges who are full of stubborn will and free spirit. They are the ones standing watch over lives undaunted. And whether or not we acknowledge their presence, they remain by our sides—always.

# Promises Kept

*For the Lord will not forsake his people;
he will not abandon his heritage.*

Psalm 94:14

Heavenly Father, thank you for
the times you've intervened
in my life through angels. They bring
the reality of your caring heart into the
reality of my days. By them, you remind
me that you have promised never to
leave me nor forsake me. Thank you for
the comfort you give through the angels
you send.

*I call upon God for comfort and solace,
and he sends me angels to answer
my plea. They gently mend my broken
heart, and I am at peace in the world
and one with heaven.*

# Help Me Do God's Work

Heavenly Father, just for today, please keep my eyes open, my hands willing, and my heart eager to help everyone in need who crosses my path—even if the need is as small as an encouraging smile and even if it requires a sacrifice of time and resources. Just for today, God. With your guidance, I have faith that, day by day, I can help more, give more, and be an earthly angel to those in need.

*When we find ourselves the agents of God's goodness to others in the course of a day, we are participating in the work of angels.*

# With God All Things Are Possible

*God is faithful, and he will not let you be tested beyond your strength, but with the testing he will also provide the way out so that you may be able to endure it.*

1 Corinthians 10:13

These hard times help me see with new eyes, Lord. Despite my tears, I see more clearly your tender mercies, my great need for your presence in my life, and the angels I had overlooked or would never have otherwise seen. Sometimes I think that I'm not strong enough to handle the tests life throws at me, but I know that with you and your angels by my side, I can do anything. Thank you for opening my eyes and healing my heart.

# Bless All the Little Children

*Children are a gift from God;*
*they are his reward.*

Psalm 127:3 TLB

I want to pray for the children in my life, Father. They're so innocent, and this world can sometimes be a harsh place. Thank you for assigning them a special place in your care and for giving their guardian angels direct access to you at all times. Be with them today and protect them—heart, mind, body, and soul. I know they will thrive in your love.

# Guide Me, Lord

*"In your steadfast love you led the people whom you redeemed; you guided them by your strength to your holy abode."*

Exodus 15:13

Help me be open to your guidance, Lord, however it comes. When you speak to me in the words of a friend, open my ears. When you hold me in the embrace of a family member, let me feel your gentle touch. And when you come to me in the almost imperceptible rush of angels' wings, alert my senses to your presence.

*Riding on the wings of angels, you can see your life from a distance and let go of the small and unimportant concerns that hold you down.*

# Speak to Me, Lord

*Open my eyes that I may see*
*wonderful things...*

Psalm 119:18 NIV

O Lord, we give thanks for your presence, which greets us each day in the guise of a friend, a work of nature, or a story from a stranger. We are reminded through these messengers in our times of deepest need that you are indeed watching over us. Lord, we have known you in the love and care of a friend, who envelops us and keeps us company in our despair. When we observe the last morning glory stretching faithfully to receive what warmth is left in the chilly sunshine, we are heartened and inspired to do the same. When we are hesitant to speak up and then read in the newspaper a story of courage and controversy, we find our voice lifted and strengthened by your message in black-and-white type. Lord, we are grateful receivers of all the angelic messages that surround us every day.

*Angels do the work of love—*
*love around us, love within us,*
*love compelling us, and love igniting us.*

# Staying Nearby

*Cast all your anxiety on him because*
*he cares for you.*

1 Peter 5:7 NIV

*I* can do it myself, I protest, but, O God, I know it's not true. Open me to your limitless love, which is found in the skillful caring of those who know firsthand my present trouble. They bring your message home and I feel you close— as close as angel wings beating gently upon my stubborn loneliness.

*Angels find us, not only when we need them most, but also when we think we are fine on our own.*

# Relinquishing Control

*And when we cried unto the Lord,*
*he heard our voice, and sent an angel,*
*and hath brought us forth…*

Numbers 20:16 KJV

God, help me to accept the help I
need and to give up my stubborn
need to control the outcome of every
situation. Show me that sometimes my
will is not always for the best, and help
me see that you send us guiding angels
in the form of other humans. Amen.

*Angels do not change your mind;*
*they wait patiently until you do.*

# Send Me an Angel

*With upright heart he tended them,*
*and guided them with skillful hand.*

Psalm 78:72

Send me an angel
To help me through my day,
For I don't think that I can take
The challenges that come my way.

I need a winged helper
To lift me from my cares
And pull me up into the light
When I'm drowning in my fears.

Give me a guardian
To hold me while I sleep
And shelter me from any harm
In mighty arms my soul to keep.

Grant me a companion
With strength to carry me along,
To give me hope when I am lost
And teach me right from wrong.

Deliver me an angel
Made especially for me,
One who'll know my deepest dreams
And guide me toward my destiny.

*In the company of angels, every problem
has a solution, every challenge has a
lesson, every cloud has a silver lining.
In the company of angels, troubles are
diminished, trials are overcome, and life
becomes a blessing again.*

# Messengers of God

*And the angel said unto them, Fear not:*
*for, behold, I bring you good tidings of*
*great joy, which shall be to all people.*

Luke 2:10 KJV

In the Bible, angels appear to a variety of people with messages appropriate to the people and their situations. If an angel were to come to you today, what message do you think you would receive?

You are truly blessed.
The Lord is with you.
Don't be afraid!

*To receive grace means that we are given*
*good things in this life, such as angels,*
*whether we deserve them or not.*

# Someone to Watch Over Me

The Lord will guide you continually, and
satisfy your needs in parched places, and
make your bones strong; and you shall be
like a watered garden, like a spring
of water, whose waters never fail.

Isaiah 58:11

*Thank you for the unseen hands that
guide my way. Thank you for the eyes that
watch my step. Thank you for the care
that keeps me safe, even when the angels
are incognito. Thank you for the trouble
I have missed even though I never saw it
coming. Every visible thing in the world is
under the charge of an angel.*

—Augustine of Hippo

# To Serve and Protect

For the Lord loves justice and fairness;
he will never abandon his people.
They will be kept safe forever;
but all who love wickedness shall perish.

Psalm 37:28 TLB

Dear God,
Thank you for those persons in uniform who watch over us and care for us. Every day, they put their lives on the line to protect, serve, and help complete strangers. Bless them, guide them in their duties, and keep them safe.

# Lead the Way!

*Consider what I say; and the Lord give thee understanding in all things.*

2 Timothy 2:7 KJV

Creator of all that exists, come to me as you have come to so many—in the guise of angels. Speak to me your message. Open my ears that I might hear your words. And give me understanding of what you would have me do.

*Here I stand at a crossroads,*
*Wondering which way I should go*
*I ask for a sign, but in my heart,*
*I believe I already know.*
*Intuition? Inspiration? No.*
*My angel told me so.*

# Applying to Be an Angel

*For this reason ... we have not stopped*
*praying for you. We continually ask God to*
*fill you with the knowledge of his will through*
*all the wisdom and understanding ...*
Colossians 1:9 NIV

God, I want to be an angel, but I'm not sure I fit the job description. I may not even meet the requirements to get hired. You may have plenty of others who could do the job better than me. But my heart is willing, and I can easily muster enthusiasm for the task ahead. I know you can work in me, so I'm asking for your spirit of encouragement—your special blessing. Help me act like an angel and ask for no reward. Let your spirit be my spirit so we can fly together!

# My Aha Moment

*Dear friends, let us practice loving each other, for love comes from God and those who are loving and kind show that they are the children of God, and that they are getting to know him better. But if a person isn't loving and kind, it shows that he doesn't know God—for God is love.*

1 John 4:7–8 TLB

*L*ord, I think I finally get it. You invest your spirit in me so that I can offer you to the world around me. Help me do this well. My hands and my heart are available to you even if I don't have wings and a halo.

65

# All Creatures Great and Small

*... ask the animals, and they will teach you;*
*the birds of the air, and they will tell you....*
*Who among all these does not know that*
*the hand of the Lord has done this? In his*
*hand is the life of every living thing and*
*the breath of every human being.*

Job 12:7, 9–10

God of all things, we thank you for all your creatures—from the largest to the smallest. In each of these wondrous animals, we see your creative touch. Protect their lives, and help us respect all you have created. Let us also be ready to learn from them anything you would like to teach us.

# Minister to My Spirit

*The Lord is good to those who wait
for him, to the soul that seeks him.
It is good that one should wait quietly for
the salvation of the Lord.*

Lamentations 3:25–26

Lord, help me keep my heart open
to the messengers of your love
that you send my way. Through them,
you minister to my needs—physical,
emotional, mental, and spiritual. Remind
me that each one is an angel—a gift from
your heart, intended to lift and support
me along my way.

67

# A Compassionate Heart

*But love your enemies, do good, and lend,
expecting nothing in return. Your reward
will be great, and you will be children
of the Most High; for he is kind to the
ungrateful and the wicked. Be merciful,
just as your Father is merciful.*

Luke 6:35–36

Never let my needs overshadow
my recognition of the needs
of others. Ground me in empathy.
Commission my sympathy. Urge me
to offer comforting hands and an
understanding heart. And in so doing,
show me how easing the pain of others
eases my own.

# Actions Speak Louder than Words

*Do to others as you would have
them do to you.*

Luke 6:31 NIV

Heavenly Father, it's easy to say,
"Let me know if there's
anything I can do." But it is much better
to peer closer, assess the situation to find
what needs doing, and then simply do it.
Help me look into a friend's needs instead
of waiting to be asked. Help me replace
the words I utter so glibly with actions
that might matter even more. Amen.

# I Can Do That

When someone needs a favor
  Or a shoulder they can cry on,
A kind word of support
Or a friend they can rely on,
I can do that.

When someone needs a helping hand
Or a bit of kind advice,
A confidante to share their dreams
Or just someone who's nice,
I can do that.

When someone cannot carry on
And I have strength to spare,
Or if they're feeling lonely
And they need someone to care,
I can do that.

When someone is afraid
And they see little hope in sight,
Or if they lose their way
And need to find a guiding light,
I can do that.

I can be an angel
To a soul in need today
Or make the going easier
For someone else's way.

*Everyone who performs a good deed is truly an angel. One doesn't need to wear feathered wings or golden halos to offer a heavenly helping hand.*

# Shared Blessings

*Don't forget to do good and to share what you have with those in need, for such sacrifices are very pleasing to him.*

Hebrews 13:16 TLB

*D*ear God, please be with all the homeless people and animals, those struggling with depression or addiction or loneliness, and those who are walking through life in a daze, not as happy as they could be. Send angels to guide them along life's journey. Please help them get whatever it is they need each and every day, whether it's food, shelter, clean drinking water, a job, a home, or a loving, supportive network of family and friends. Please let them always be treated with the love, compassion, dignity, and respect that they deserve. And please point them in the right direction to get the help they need to feel the love and joy that you want all your children to experience. Thank you. Amen.

*Angels look for the best in us and then they nourish that place. They see a vision of whom God has created us to be and they dream that dream with us.*

# Light My Way

*For we know that if the earthly tent
we live in is destroyed, we have a building
from God, an eternal house in heaven,
not built by human hands.*

2 Corinthians 5:1 NIV

Father, hold us in your arms in
the midst of devastation and
ruin. Remind us that rampaging nature
and human evil will not touch us in
our eternal homes. Send your angels to
remind us that our lives and homes on
earth are part of the journey, not our
final destination. Amen.

*Sometimes hope seems as unreal as
the angel beside you. But both are real.*

# Faith Versus Fear

*Bless the Lord, ye his angels, that excel in strength, that do his commandments, hearkening unto the voice of his word.*

Psalm 103:20 KJV

*L*oving Lord, you have sent angels to your people on earth throughout history. Some brought messages of hope, others gave warning. Some angels helped still fearful hearts or encourage the downtrodden. Thank you for always being there.

*In the most important moments of humanity, angels have served as holy commentators, announcing the good news of new life and resurrection. With women and men, angels have celebrated the wonder of God's redemption.*

# Courage and Strength

*These troubles and sufferings of ours are,*
*after all, quite small and won't last very*
*long.... So we do not look at what we*
*can see right now, the troubles all around*
*us, but we look forward to the joys in*
*heaven which we have not yet seen.*
*The troubles will soon be over, but*
*the joys to come will last forever.*

2 Corinthians 4:17–18 TLB

*Y*ou know, Lord, lately I have been
struggling just to get through
the next hour, the next minute, and the
next second. Be merciful to me in my
weakness and bring me strength and
encouragement through the angels you
send. They are faithful messengers of
your compassion and comfort. Amen.

# Take My Hand

*For all who are led by the Spirit of God*
*are children of God.*

Romans 8:14

God, I am a child no longer, yet I still know the need to have someone take me by the hand and lead me out of a scary place. Throughout my life, you've sent those people to me, and together we have found the way. Bless those angels, Lord. May they find the hands to hold when they need them. Amen.

*If you pray truly, you will feel within*
*yourself a great assurance, and the angels*
*will be your companions.*

—Evagrius of Pontus

# Listen for God's Voice

Lord, you come to us in the storm, the fire, and even in the stillness of a quiet moment. Sometimes your message is strong, carried on bustling angelic wings. Sometimes our spirits are nudged, our hearts lightened by the gentle whisper of angel voices. However you approach us, your message is always one of tender love and compassion. Thank you for the certainty—and the surprise— of your holy voice.

*May you always experience the presence of angels in your daily life so that you may have peace, comfort, and hope for the future.*

# Travel Companions

Whenever you take a journey—whether across town to a familiar destination or across the country to a new place—remember to take an angel with you. The angel will guide your path, watch your steps, and keep you company along the way.

*We never travel alone.*
*Invisible angels surround us,*
*walking with us on our journey,*
*quietly sustaining our spirits and pouring*
*love over us with the lightness of air.*
*And we don't even hear*
*the rustling of their wings.*

# There's an Angel in All of Us

*Dear brothers and sisters... Be joyful.*
*Grow to maturity. Encourage each other.*
*Live in harmony and peace. Then the God*
*of love and peace will be with you.*

2 Corinthians 13:11 NLT

An angel reached out and took my finger today and squeezed it as tight as a baby can squeeze. An angel smiled at me from her wheelchair. An angel sheltered me from the rain and helped me get into the office without getting wet. You may call them a baby, a senior citizen, or a good Samaritan, but they are the angels that watch out for me every day, making my life more comfortable and my awareness more real.

# God's Majestic Creations

*How many are your works, Lord!*
*In wisdom you made them all;*
*the earth is full of your creatures.*

Psalm 104:24 NIV

Father God, the earth is asleep. The buds of spring lie in wait. The wonder of your world seems to be in a holding pattern, just waiting for the go-ahead to grow. Let winter teach us the value of stillness, silence, and meditation. Help us know that angel wings don't have to flutter wildly to do the work of your kingdom of peace.

# Let Me Hear Your Message

*But don't just listen to God's word. You must do what it says. Otherwise, you are only fooling yourselves.*

James 1:22 NLT

od of all words and of the angels, I kneel before you in wonder at the ways you speak to me. Help me hear your message in words, in deeds, in thoughts, in relationships, and in nature. Let me, in all things and at all times, be open to your message for my life.

*Angels carry messages from heaven to earth. God uses his angels to tell us of his mercy and to show us where he wants us to go.*

# Angels of Comfort

*And the angel of the Lord said to her,*
*"...the Lord has given heed to your*
*affliction."*

Genesis 16:11

Our hearts are bruised, Father—black and blue from life's pounding, swollen and sore from hurts real and imagined. We need a soothing balm to ease our discomfort. Please send into our lives angelic beings who have healing hands and helping hearts, those who would ease our pain by word and deed. Amen.

*No heart is so heavy and no soul is so bleak that they can't be lifted by the wings of angels.*

# A Prayer About Angels

Lord, open my eyes that I might see a whole new level of reality. When I feel overwhelmed by my problems, show me your angelic army all around me. Thank you for the tenacious way they guard me, keeping me from potential harm that I may never even know about. Let me join my voice with theirs in praising you: the holy one, the worthy one, the victor over all in heaven and earth. Glory to you in the highest, Lord, and peace in my little world. Amen.

*Faith is to believe what we do not see, and the reward of this faith is to see what we believe.*

—Augustine of Hippo

# God's Steadfast Love

*O give thanks to the Lord, for he is good,*
*for his steadfast love endures forever.*

Psalm 136:1

God, you love us more than we can
ever comprehend. You have even
given your angels charge over us, to
guide and protect us. Help us be worthy
of your love and the angels' care, so that
those we meet might consider us bearers
of angelic love.

*In the mysterious, unexplained events*
*of our lives, we sense the hand of an*
*intervening angel to remind us of the*
*reality of God's ever-present love.*

# Friends Are Worry Erasers

*Don't worry about anything; instead, pray about everything; tell God your needs and don't forget to thank him for his answers. If you do this you will experience God's peace, which is far more wonderful than the human mind can understand. His peace will keep your thoughts and your hearts quiet and at rest as you trust in Christ Jesus.*

Philippians 4:6–7 TLB

*G*od, when my heart is filled with worry, you never fail to send a friend into my life to lift my spirits. Whether it's an email with a funny picture, a phone call, or a visit for coffee, my friends always seem to know when I need their love and presence the most. True friends are angels in disguise, and I am so thankful for the old and new friends you have sent to help me when I most need a little extra light. I pray I will always be there for them when they need me as well.

*Nothing helps alleviate worry better than a visit from a supportive and caring friend who knows just what to say and do to make you feel on top of the world again.*

# Someone Else's Angel

*Dear friends, since God loved us as much as that, we surely ought to love each other too. For though we have never yet seen God, when we love each other God lives in us and his love within us grows ever stronger.*

1 John 4:11–12 TLB

God, with health and financial and relationship issues, I've been so focused on myself and my problems lately that it's no wonder I feel alone, lost, and adrift. I ask that you help me to climb out of myself for a little while and be of help to another. Perhaps by making someone else feel accepted, loved,

and cared for, I will be lifted out of my own life just long enough to feel more connected and less alone. Help me see the big picture of this puzzle called my life instead of being so intensely focused on each piece. God, help me to be an angel to others and to relight my own heart in doing so.

*If I can put one touch of rosy sunset into the life of any man or woman, I shall feel that I have worked with God.*
—G. K. Chesterton

# Shine a Light

*The Lord is near to all who call on him....*
*He fulfills the desire of all who fear him;*
*he also hears their cry, and saves them.*
*The Lord watches over all who love him...*

Psalm 145:18–20

Dear God, I need a host of angels to pull me out of this swamp of sorrow and the unrelenting darkness of grief. Please send your angels to shine their light on the beauty of your creation so I can have a few moments of joy today. Tomorrow may be easier, but I really do need as many angels as you can spare today. Thank you. Amen.

*Angels help lead us out of darkness and into God's light.*

# Always by My Side

*"Because he loves me,"* says the Lord,
*"I will rescue him; I will protect him,*
*for he acknowledges my name.*
*He will call on me, and I will answer him;*
*I will be with him in trouble,*
*I will deliver him and honor him."*

Psalm 91:14–15 NIV

Heavenly Father—
I want to thank you for the angels who are always there for me in times of trouble, as well as times of joy. I know I can always turn to them to deliver your wisdom and comfort, no matter what is going on in my life. I am so grateful for their blessed presence, which surrounds me with love and fills me with peace.

91

# Facing Forward

*I consider that the sufferings of this
present time are not worth comparing with
the glory about to be revealed to us.*

Romans 8:18

*L*ord, I treasure my family, for when
things are at their worst, they are
at their best, supporting and loving me
like a band of precious angels sent from
above. I've been dealing with some heavy-
duty challenges lately, but my family is
always there when I need them, and they
always know when I need some quiet
time. With the family you have blessed
me with, I know I can stay focused on

the brighter days ahead and keep my face turned toward the sun, even when it seems so dark. My family keeps me real. Thank you, Lord, for giving them to me.

*The future is so much brighter when you let others help and support you during your darkest hours. The people who love you are servants of God sent to earth to remind you of how special and precious you are.*

# Living in Gratitude

*The Lord, your God, is in your midst, a warrior who gives victory; he will rejoice over you with gladness, he will renew you in his love; he will exult over you with loud singing as on a day of festival.*

Zephaniah 3:17–18

God, when I least expected it today, you sent me an angel in the form of a caring stranger who made my day a little brighter and a little warmer. It was nothing big—just a pleasant smile and some small talk that reminded me that friendly people are everywhere and that I may learn something from a random conversation with someone I've never met before. I am amazed at your consistent and persistent miracles, big and small. If I don't say thank you enough, please forgive me, God. I truly am grateful!

*Miracles can be found in every corner if we have the grateful eyes to see them. When we live in a state of gratitude, we are rewarded with more and more things to be grateful for.*

# I Thought I Met an Angel

I thought I heard an angel
Whisper in my ear,
Telling me which way to go
And that she'd guide me there.

I thought I felt a wisp of a wing
Brush against my arm,
Surrounding me with loving grace
To keep me safe from harm.

I thought I saw an angel
Dancing through the air,
Spreading joy to all below
Who called to God in prayer.

I thought I met an angel
In a loving, caring friend,
There for me through thick and thin,
Loyal 'til the end.

I thought I touched an angel
In the arms of one I love,
Enfolded in the gentle glow
Of blessings from above.

# Your Ways
# Are My Ways

*Make me to know your ways, O Lord;
teach me your paths. Lead me in your
truth, and teach me, for you are
the God of my salvation; for you
I wait all day long.*

Psalm 25:4–5

Lord, I thank you for the teachers
you have sent into my life. Some
have hurt me and some have helped me,
but all have been instrumental in making
me who I am today. I believe they are all
angels sent to challenge me to think in
higher ways and live a more authentic

life. Even those people whom I have felt anger toward have left me with lessons that have helped me to grow and become a more kind and loving person. I thank you for using others as my earthbound angels to help me be the best I can be.

*Every person who graces our lives has something to offer. Some may offer lessons, some may just be blessings, but all are angels sent to make us more than we were before.*

# The Power of Forgiveness

*Be gentle and ready to forgive;*
*never hold grudges. Remember,*
*the Lord forgave you,*
*so you must forgive others.*

Colossians 3:13 TLB

God, I don't pretend to be perfect.
I make mistakes. I screw up. I say
and do things that hurt other people.
Let my guardian angel walk with me
today and gently remind me to stop and
think about what I am doing and saying
before I act. I know that you forgive me
for my foibles, but I would like the

guidance and patience to stop making so many of them. Let me forgive myself, as well as those who have wronged me, so we can all treat each other with more kindness, compassion, and dignity. Amen.

*Angels see us much differently than we see ourselves. We so often concentrate on our weaknesses and our faults. But angels see us from the inside out because they view us through the love of God.*

# Refocus My Attention

*Take delight in the Lord, and he will*
*give you the desires of your heart.*

Psalm 37:4 NIV

*L*ord, I've been feeling really down lately. Forgive me if I don't seem grateful for all the blessings you bestow on me each and every day. I truly am appreciative, but right now, I'm having a difficult time focusing on what I *do* have rather than the things that I'm longing for. Please let my guardian angels lift me out of these blues and carry me through this dark time. Help them fill me with faith that you will provide for all my heart's desires. Thank you. Amen.

# Divine Protection

*L*ord in heaven,
Please help me to see the angels
whom I know you have placed in my
presence. Help me to slow down and
know that I am always divinely protected
and guided. Help me to spread your
word, do your work, be kind, and love.
Thank you, Lord, for your help this day.

*An angel doesn't have to speak
to be heard, be visible to be seen,
or be present to be felt.
Believe in angels
and they will always be near.*

# The Child Inside Guides the Way

*[Jesus said,] "Truly I tell you, unless you change and become like children, you will never enter the kingdom of heaven. Whoever becomes humble like this child is the greatest in the kingdom of heaven."*

Matthew 18:3–4

*D*ear Lord, help me find the child inside me again. That child is my own inner angel, urging me to slow down and smell the roses. I work so hard for my family and often forget the joy and wonder of just being alive and playing.

Help me to see that joy is the greatest gift and that I don't always have to bury myself in work and obligations to feel that I am a good, worthy person. Bring out the child in me today, Lord, and give me wings. Let me see life through the fresh eyes of awe and wonder again, happy and without a care in the world.

*Life is not just about work and making a living. It's about being alive and letting our hearts sing and dance and enjoy the fruits of our labor. Let yourself be merry for a while... the work will always be there.*

# Superpowers Activate!

*The Lord is the everlasting God, the Creator of the ends of the earth....He gives power to the faint, and strengthens the powerless....those who wait for the Lord shall renew their strength,...they shall run and not be weary, they shall walk and not faint.*

Isaiah 40:28–29, 31

God, sometimes I feel like a superhero. Taking care of a family, working for a living, fixing this boo-boo, solving that problem, and trying to find time for myself has me feeling like I should be wearing wings or a cape. Help me rise to the occasion of being an amazing angel and hero for others when I can. And also help me find quiet time for myself so I can get up and do it all again tomorrow. Keep me focused on what counts and strong enough to overcome the little things that zap my energy and spirit so I can handle the bigger things. I know others count on me, but I can only do so much without your help.

*God will always step in and do for us what we cannot do for ourselves.*

# Our Angels

They flutter, they flicker,
They flash and they fly.
They skim along, soar above,
And sail through the sky.
They dart and they dance,
They dash all around.
They hover and sweep,
Not making a sound.
They plunge and they launch,
They sail like a breeze.
They worship and tremble
And fall on their knees.
They rescue, they liberate,
They guard and preserve.

They give us protection,
They give us the nerve
To stand a bit taller,
To trust a bit more,
To face disappointment
With both feet on the floor,
To revere and to hope
In a place they call home,
To live with the knowledge
That we're never alone.

# You Light Up My Life

*Let love be genuine…*
*love one another with mutual affection;*
*outdo one another in showing honor.*

Romans 12:9–10

I've been blessed with a love so deep and true. My husband—my best friend, companion, and angel—is always by my side on the path of life. Thank you, God, for bringing into my world a light and a love so wonderful. Help me to always treat this person with compassion, warmth, and kindness so that our love will last a lifetime. I know people don't always get the chance to marry their best friend, but you have given me that chance, and I hope to never squander it. Help me be the best wife I can be and to always do my share of the loving and giving.

*Finding a true soul mate is like having your own special angel to walk life's path with.*

# Be a Do-Gooder!

Lord, let me be an angel for someone today. I know how good it feels to have someone do something good for me, and I tend to get so self-involved that I often forget to pay it forward. Help me to find opportunities to be of help to people, no matter how big or small the acts might be. Remind me to smile, hold doors open, and make small talk that we humans seem to do so little of lately. Help me help others remember that we all need each other. The world can be such a cold place; let me spread a little warmth today!

# A Friend in Need

*I give you a new commandment, that you love one another. Just as I have loved you, you also should love one another.*

John 13:34

Dear God,
A special friend of mine is hurting right now. He's going through a difficult time, and he needs encouragement. I pray that you'll heal his aching heart and soothe his soul. May your loving angels guide him in the right direction and pull him out of his grief and sadness. Help him find the happiness and love that he deserves. Please help me always be there for him to laugh and to cry and to offer him love and support.

# Be My Guide

*The people who walked in darkness
have seen a great light; those who lived
in a land of deep darkness—on them
light has shined.*

Isaiah 9:2

Excuse me, God, but it's pretty dark in here right now. If it's not too much trouble, I could sure use an angel or two to help me see what's going on. Just a little help to get me moving in the right direction would be so very much appreciated. I know the dawn is coming. I'm just not sure which direction to turn to find it. Thanks!

*When it's too dark to see your path,
trust your angels to guide you.*

# Letting Go of the Past

*For I know the plans I have for you, says the Lord. They are plans for good and not for evil, to give you a future and a hope.*

Jeremiah 29:11 TLB

Dear God,
Thank you for sending your angels to give me the courage and strength to let go of the past so that I could move on with my life and embrace all the amazing things you have planned for me. I'm so grateful that you gave me the power to forgive those who have hurt me in the past so that I could be free to give and receive love with a whole heart. Thank you for being patient with me. Amen.

# The Blessings in the Lessons

*"In everything do to others as you would have them do to you; for this is the law and the prophets."*

Matthew 7:12

od, I know that we are all created in your image, so I hope to always be a positive role model. I know that is a tall order, so when I fall short, help me have the same compassion for myself as I have for those who don't always treat me properly. Just as others often act as angels for me, I would like to do the same for them. Let me be someone else's wings today.

*Some of our most significant teachers come to us in the form of difficult people who press our buttons, vex our spirits, and get on our nerves. But these people act as mirrors to expose the negative traits that we dislike in ourselves. Learn from these people. They are a gift.*

# What Really Lasts

*Do you want to be truly rich?*
*You already are if you are happy and good.*
*After all, we didn't bring any money with*
*us when we came into the world,*
*and we can't carry away a single penny*
*when we die.*

1 Timothy 6:6–7 TLB

God, you have blessed me with children who keep my heart light and free. You have blessed me with elderly relatives who provide guidance and understanding, for they have been through every storm that now faces me. You have blessed me with friends who offer shoulders to lean on or cry on, whatever I may need. I am surrounded by angels of every size, color, shape, and age, and I am forever grateful for these amazing treasures you have bestowed upon me. Thank you, God.

*When life on earth is ending, people don't surround themselves with objects. What we want around us is people—people we love and have relationships with.*

—Rick Warren

# Angels of Hope and Faith

*Be glad for all God is planning for you.*
*Be patient . . . and prayerful always.*

Romans 12:12 TLB

*L*ord, thank you for blessing me with angels who have taught me to have faith and hope and to trust in your will and your timing. It's not always easy to be patient or to relinquish control, but I'm grateful that you've allowed me to put my worries and desires in your hands, trusting that you know what's best for me. Thank you to my angels for taking my hand and guiding me each step of the way.

# A Prayer for Healing

*In my desperation I prayed, and the Lord listened; he saved me from all my troubles. For the angel of the Lord is a guard; he surrounds and defends all who fear him.*

Psalm 34:6–7 NLT

Lord, you made me; you can fix me. You put my body together. You knitted my nerves. You wrote my DNA. You taught me how to laugh and how to love. Something's wrong now—the system's crashing. I trust you to make it better. But what does "better" mean? Healthy, yes, but also whole again. Body, mind, feelings in balance, relationships in sync, my spirit soaring with yours. Lord, you created me and called your creation good. Make me whole again, please. Amen.

# Home Is Where Your Heart Is

*"Do not let your hearts be troubled.
Believe in God, believe also in me.
In my Father's house there are many
dwelling places."*

John 14:1–2

How blessed I am, God, to have such a wonderful place to call home, with such wonderful people in my life, and to be surrounded by such wonderful things. My home is like heaven on earth, filled with specially chosen angels that accompany me on this amazing journey called life. I feel

safe, secure, and loved here, and I am so blessed to have a place to live and dream that brings out the best in me and all who walk through these doors. Thank you, God, for my beautiful home—my little slice of heaven.

*When we dwell in love and gratitude, any place we go becomes our home. For our true home is within us, where our hearts live.*

# An Abundant Life

*"Do not be afraid, little flock,
for it is your Father's good pleasure to
give you the kingdom."*

Luke 12:32

God, I just want to take a little time out from my day to thank you for the abundance all around me. There was a time when all I saw was what I lacked, but you have taught me to see blessings in everything and angels in every being I encounter. I am so thankful to be surrounded by proof of your love and grace. There are times when I may not have all I want, but I always have all I need, and that makes me feel safe and loved and at peace. Amen.

*To see proof of God's abundance, simply go outside and try to count the blades of grass in a field.*

# Angels All Around Us

There are angels all around us,
No one is ever alone,
Even in our darkest hour,
Our deepest needs are known.
There are angels all around us,
Though seldom can we see,
The guardians among us,
Watching over you and me.

There are angels all around us,
Hidden barely out of sight,
Waiting for the moment when
The time to give is right.
If you listen then your heart may hear
The rustle of angel wings
Or catch a glimmer of a halo's glow,
A hint that angels are real things.

There are angels all around us.
They wipe away our tears.
They tend to our breaking hearts,
Our pain, our grief, our fears.
There are angels all around us,
Though we rarely get to see
The angels all around us,
Watching over you and me.

**Acknowledgments:**

Unless otherwise noted, all scripture quotations are taken from the *New Revised Standard Version* of the Bible. Copyright © 1989 by the Division of Christian Education of the National Council of the Churches of Christ in the United States of America. Used by permission. All rights reserved.

Scripture quotations marked KJV are taken from *The Holy Bible, King James Version*. Copyright © 1977, 1984, Thomas Nelson Inc., Publishers.

Scripture quotations marked NIV are taken from *The Holy Bible, New International Version*®, NIV®. Copyright © 1973, 1978, 1984, 2011 by Biblica, Inc.™ Used by permission of Zondervan. All rights reserved worldwide.

Scripture quotations marked NLT are taken from *The Holy Bible, New Living Translation*, copyright © 1996, 2004, 2007 by Tyndale House Foundation. Used by permission of Tyndale House Publishers, Inc., Carol Stream, Illinois, 60188. All rights reserved.

Scripture quotations marked TLB are taken from *The Living Bible*, copyright © 1971. Used by permission of Tyndale House Publishers, Inc., Carol Stream, Illinois, 60188. All rights reserved.

**Cover Art:** Shutterstock.com

**Interior Art:** Shutterstock.com